LETTERS
TO THE
MOON

BRITTANY SCHROEDER

Letters to the Moon

Copyright © 2025 by Brittany Schroeder.

All rights reserved. No part of this publication may be reproduced, distributed, or transmitted in any form or by any means, including photocopying, recording, or other electronic or mechanical methods, without the written consent of the publisher. The only exceptions are for brief quotations included in critical reviews and other noncommercial uses permitted by copyright law.

MILTON & HUGO L.L.C.
4407 Park Ave., Suite 5
Union City, NJ 07087, USA

Website: *www. miltonandhugo.com*
Hotline: *1- 888-778-0033*
Email: *info@miltonandhugo.com*

Ordering Information:
Quantity sales. Special discounts are granted to corporations, associations, and other organizations. For more information on these discounts, please reach out to the publisher using the contact information provided above.

Library of Congress Control Number:	2025901791	
ISBN-13:	979-8-89285-433-7	[Paperback Edition]
	979-8-89285-434-4	[Digital Edition]

Rev. date: 01/30/2025

In loving memory of Case. Thank you for supporting my dreams and making me believe they could one day come true. Your belief in me made me believe in myself. Rest in peace, my love.

To my best friends, Steven, Sydney, and Justin, thank you for never giving up on me. Your constant support and encouragement mean the absolute world to me.

I would not be here without any of you. From the bottom of my heart, thank you. This is for you.

I got tired of screaming, so I started writing

FOR THEM

Writing is my escape
From the darkness that surrounds
It frees me from the hell
That occupies my mind

I can scream
And cry
And bare my soul
Without ever making a sound

It's kept me alive
Reminded me to breathe
And helped me realize
That I'm not alone

If my pain
And my experiences
Can save the life of someone like me
Then I write for them

SHE IS ME

She was 14
14 when you started noticing her
14 when you said hello
14 when you said you liked her

She believed you
When you said she was a good kind of different
When you said she made you happy
When you said you loved her

Then she was 15
15 when you asked her out
15 when you made her feel alive
15 when you took advantage

She was terrified
She was confused
She was uncomfortable
She was violated

She said no
But you shushed her
She said stop
But you didn't

Now she's broken
She blames herself
She feels like she shouldn't have ever said hello back
But she can't change the past

She regrets never turning you in
She still sees you in her nightmares
She doesn't look at love the way she used to
And she's afraid of getting too close

She was young
You ruined her
She'll never be the same girl
She is me

SOMETHING I NEVER WANTED TO ADMIT

Fear
Violated
Pain
These are all the things I felt

You used me
You hurt me
You assaulted me
You made me feel worthless

I wanted to die
I felt dirty in my own skin
Nothing I did could fix it
I hated who I saw in the mirror

I felt broken
Betrayed
Unloved
And unimportant

I tried to hide it
I wished for this to just go away
I never wanted anybody to find out
But what I wanted isn't what I got

One question
"Did he touch you?"
I couldn't stop the tears
Or the shaking of my body

That one question
Turned my world upside down
It was like I was reliving the moment
And I felt sick

I remember nodding my head
It was as if words ceased to exist
And in that very moment
I wished to die

I didn't want to live
Knowing that somebody else knew
About the things you did to me
I hated it

I had wanted to take this secret to my grave
I wanted to pretend it didn't happen
I didn't want to talk about it
And I didn't want to report it

After people started finding out
They would ask me why I didn't report you
Why didn't I make you pay for what you did
I'll tell you

This world is cruel
I didn't want to become the talk of the town
I didn't want fingers pointed in my direction
I didn't want hushed voices every where I went

I didn't want to be blamed for what happened
I didn't want to have to explain myself
I was only 15
I just wanted to move forward

But I couldn't
You haunted my dreams
And made it impossible
For me to forget

I just wanted to be loved
I thought you would respect me
But you took my innocence
And you stomped on it

You made me hate myself
You made me broken
You made me feel less than human
You made me the victim

HELP ME

I don't eat very much
I don't sleep much anymore
I don't laugh like I used to
I don't quite smile like before

I'm distant
I'm disconnected
I'm tired
"I'm okay"

I've dropped every hint
I've shown all the signs
I've done everything I can think of
So tell me

What do you expect from me
What more do I need to do
Just how loud do I need to scream
Before you realize I'm drowning

ME NEITHER

Do you know that feeling?
When the world comes to life
And the wind and animals
Seem to sing to you

That feeling when happiness takes over
And you can't believe you got this lucky
You look forward to each passing day
Because each day brings new memories

The feeling when you laugh and smile
Because you feel blessed
That you woke up
And get to live another day

Do you know that feeling?
The feeling of true happiness
...
Me neither

YOU BROKE ME

Yelling
Screaming
Slamming doors
Anger

You're angry
I don't like it when you're angry
You turn mean
And hurtful

No friends?
No going out with family?
No trips?
No doing anything without you?

Fine
I'll do whatever you want
Just please don't hurt me
Not again

You threatened to kill me
You were drunk
I believed every word
I still do

I have nightmares sometimes
I'm afraid of running into you
I can never fully relax
I'm always on high alert

It's been years now
Since I escaped from your grasp
But our past still haunts me
And I can't shake the fear that you're still angry

KEYWORD: YET..

"I'm fine"
A desperate call for help
A cover up
A lie

Darkness sets in
Not only on the world around me
But inside as well
It's soul consuming

Someone please help
Find a light to shine in this darkness
So that there is something to give comfort and hope
Because I am deathly afraid

I know what the darkness can do
It possesses the minds of the weak
And shreds their souls
Until it is too late

The wounds in their heart
Begin to show on their skin
And the pain brings the slightest bit of comfort knowing
I'm not dead yet

WHAT IF

As I sit here in the dark
My mind wanders off
Into the unknown silence
It's all too familiar

I can't help but think
About my life
And the things I've been through
It's a living hell

And as I continue to sit here
I start thinking
About life without me
What it would be like

Would people miss me?
Would people think about me everyday?
Would people cry at the very mention of my name?
Would I mean something?

What if I had succeeded at ending it?
What if I hadn't woken up?
What if I was gone?
What would people do?

Sometimes I think
People would do nothing
Because why would they?
I'm just me

What if I don't matter?
What if I never did?
What if I never will?
What if...

YOU WERE MINE

I felt guilty
I felt broken
I felt confused
I felt as though my world was crumbling

I would have put you first
Made sure you were cared for
And had everything you could ever need
I would have given you the world

You existed and disappeared
All in the same moment
I grieved for you
Something I never thought I wanted

I loved you so much
I still do
You were mine
Even if only for a moment

February 21, 2019
Rest in peace my angel
I'm so sorry
That I didn't know

STUCK

I have never felt so lost
So far behind
I feel incomplete
And lonely

Every person I know
Is moving forward
Yet I'm stuck
In this constant state of the unknown

They all have it
At least somewhat figured out
Me?
Not even a little bit

I thought I did
I thought I knew
What my future would hold
I was wrong

One moment
Shattered it all
Now I'm here
Motionless

I'm expected to start over
Move on with life
But how?
I don't know where to start

My world was shattered
Yet I'm supposed to pretend
As though nothing happened
And walk a path I never even considered

I have no idea what I'm doing
I'm trapped
And I'm afraid
There's only one way out

I'M DROWNING

What could I have possibly done
To deserve this fate
A life like mine
Will I ever escape

THIS IS ME

Trapped
I'm trapped inside my own mind
Tormented and abused
By the thoughts and emotions that live there

Constantly fighting myself
Always trying to please those around me
I'm not happy
I want to be happy

Maybe I should just say fuck it
Do all the things they disagree with
Why have I let someone else
Tell me how to live my life

I want to be open
I want to be free
I want to love
I want to live

So here it goes
I no longer care what you think
I am proud of who I am
This is me

NO ONE KNOWS

I am confused
I am angry
I am broken
I am tired

I live a life
Where I smile and laugh
To hide my broken soul
So I don't burden anybody

I conceal the pain
To keep you smiling
Because I don't want you to know
How deep it really goes

I wish someone would notice
And see right through the walls I've built
But at the same time
I hate when people ask if I'm okay

Of course I'm not okay
My body is alive
But my mind and soul
Died long ago

I can't do this
I can't live
But I can't die either
I'm stuck

I'm stuck in a state of numbness
A feeling I can only describe as nothingness
Feeling empty
Down to your core

So don't you dare
Pretend to know how I feel
We all have our own battles
But no one knows the war I'm fighting

HOMESICK

I love you
I've loved you since the 7th grade
All the times I would come to visit
All the jokes we shared together

I love everything about you
I love the way you smile when you think I'm being cute
I love the way you hold me in your arms as you sleep
I love the way you get excited when I ask questions about things you're interested in

I miss you
I miss our life together
I miss waking up to you
I miss home

I miss your laugh
And your smile
I miss your warm embrace
And your comforting presence

I wish I could change things
I wish life had been worth the fight
I wish I could have helped you
I wish for just one more chance

I love you
I miss you
I am homesick
For a place I cannot return to

TRUTHS OF A BROKEN HEART

Love is patient, love is kind
And while that may be true
There's another side of love
I want to share with you

Love, it can be beautiful
And put joy on every face
But in my world it's different
Love left an empty space

Love is pain, love is goodbye
These truths in my heart ache
For on this day and every day
Love, to me, is heartbreak

So I may never reach my hand
Out to touch another
If again I have to love and lose
Then alone is how I'll suffer

I'd rather spend my days and nights
Just me, myself, and I
Than to ever have to once again
Say that last goodbye

FOR YOU

As the darkness washes over me
And my heart and soul die once again
There's one question that haunts me
Why do I live?

Giving up would be so easy
No more pain
No more suffocating from my own thoughts
Why do I live?

If I just disappeared
I wouldn't have to live this way anymore
I wouldn't have to bear this any longer
Why do I live?

But the pain would become someone else's
Someone who cared
Someone who loved me
It would be selfish

So to answer the question
Why do I live?
It's not for me
It's for you

FREE

Life at twenty two
Is something I never thought I'd experience
I never planned to live this long
I wasn't prepared

But life has its twisted ways
Of showing me I'm meant to live
I wasn't meant to die
When I desperately tried to

I just wish
That it was easier
To breathe
To live

I wish I could remember
What it feels like to be okay
I want to be free of the sorrows that bind me
And tell me I'll never make it out alive

HOME IS WHO HOLDS MY HEART

Your eyes
Say all the words unspoken
As you lay your gaze upon me
Drawing me in
To your embrace

The sound of your heart beating
Hypnotizing and serene
Removes me from reality
And places me in a world
Created by the warmth of you

As I lay my head
Against your chest
I am reminded
That the world can be bright
And beautiful

I find myself hoping
That moments like these
Can last forever
Just me and you
Until the end

Home
This is it
And this is what it feels like
To love
And to be loved in return

DREAMING OF HOME

As the world grows quiet
The day turns to night
And the moon shines its light on the world below
She lies in bed waiting
For his return

Her every thought
Is consumed by him
From the way his hair blows in the breeze
Or how his brown eyes shimmer in the sunlight
Revealing flecks of gold

The sound of a door unlocking
Brings her out of her trance
And the breeze from outside
Carries the scent of mahogany and pine
Straight into the bedroom

As she sits up and turns to face the door
She is greeted by the sight of him
His arms outstretched
Inviting her in
To his warm embrace

She runs to him
With a smile on her face
And he mirrors her expression
But just as she reaches him
He's gone

She awakes with a jolt
Suddenly reminded of the harsh reality
She continues to wait for him
But he can only return to her
In her dreams

END

I can't breathe
Grief and heartache consume me
Darkness surrounds
And I'm suffocating

I'm scared
For I know how deep the darkness goes
I know the demons that lurk
And I fear the battle I face

I am weak
I am tired
I am lost
I am broken

Someone help me
I can't win this on my own
The pain is slowly killing me
And my end is drawing near

GREETINGS FOR A GOODBYE

Why am I forced
To wait for death
Is it really so shameful
To reach out my hand
To greet the grim reaper

GONE

Gone
In the blink of an eye
You were just gone
You ceased to exist

Nothing can explain the pain
Or the sound of my shattering heart
I knew in those moments
Life would never be the same

Days and nights seemed to blend together
Into a never ending cycle of nothingness
I felt numb
I felt dejected

I wanted you back
I cried desperately for your return
But I knew it would never come
And that only made the pain worse

There are so many things
You never got to see
Things I accomplished
That you weren't there for

I miss you every day
I wish I could call you
Or hug you again
Instead I stare at your pictures and cry

I want to tell you
That I love you
And from deep within my soul
I hope you're proud of me

ONLY FOR YOU

I wish I could hate you
I wish I could be angry with you
But I understand on too deep of a level
The decision that you made

You wanted me to choose life
When you couldn't do the same
You put so much effort into saving my life
And I really wish you hadn't

But you knew
You knew it wasn't enough to save yourself
So you gave me everything
You knew you couldn't save us both

So you chose me
And I'll never understand why
But I won't let your efforts be in vain
Even when the last thing I want to do is keep going

I'll do it for you

WHEN WE CAN MEET AGAIN

You whisper softly in my ear
As my dream takes me away
Far from this reality
Where you no longer exist

I can see your face
And hear your voice so clearly
Your smile and your laugh
I could stay here forever

Just as suddenly
As I'm transported to this dreamworld
I am ripped away from it
Forced to face the cruel reality

You are not here
You can never come back to me here
I can only wait for you
In my dreams

When the sun takes its rest
And the stars kiss the sky
We can live the life we dreamed of
Together inside my dreams

Don't you worry my love
I will wait for you here until the end
And if an afterlife exists
I promise I will find you there

GRIEF

Grief consumes me
I'm enveloped in darkness
Is this the end?
I don't see a way out

There's no light in the distance
No glimmer of hope
That I just might make it out
Alive

The screams inside are deafening
The pain radiates through every cell in my body
Is this what it feels like?
Death without dying

You were my person
My best friend
My soulmate
The other half of my heart

What am I supposed to do?
How do I live without you?
Why did you leave me?
I don't want to live this way..

I don't want to hurt
I don't want to feel suffocating sadness
I don't want to live in any world
If you're not in it

I'm overwhelmed by emotion
Yet feel so numb
I want to scream and cry
And fight the world

I don't know if I'm strong enough to fight this
I need you
I miss you
I love you

MEMORY OF YOU

I'm okay
But I'm not okay
I can't give up
Even though I want to

I smile and I cry
It's become my daily routine
The ache in my chest
Feels like a part of me now

I find myself more tired than usual
Yet sleep is still my enemy
I find myself hungry all the time
But my appetite betrays me

I find myself giving in
To the decisions my body makes for me
Food seems overwhelming
And sleep I want to avoid

I find you in my dreams
But lose you all over again when I wake
I am both haunted and blessed
By the memory of you

SILENCE

I remember
The whispers
The screams
The cries

I remember everything
Every bit and every piece
Of that dreadful day
After you left

I couldn't breathe
The pain was overwhelming
So I sat there
And cried until I couldn't

I didn't want to live this life anymore
Especially without you
I was afraid
I am afraid

I'm afraid I'll lose the sound of your voice
And the sound of the pure happiness in your laugh
I fear a day where I will no longer be able to hear you
And all I'll hear is silence

MY CURSE

I don't trust anybody
When they say they won't leave
Everybody leaves
That's just what they do

A MASK OF BROKEN PIECES

I am angry
Angry that you left
Angry that you never said goodbye
I am angry that I wasn't given the chance
To love you longer

This anger consumes me
It eats at my very soul
Why can't I calm it?
Why won't it weaken?
Why am I so angry?

You left me here
To navigate this world without you
But I understand
I understand you wanted peace
But what about me?

I tried so hard to keep you here
And as I sit here writing this
I realize that my anger
Is just my pain
Confused and wearing a mask

I am hurt
Hurt that you left
Hurt that you never said goodbye
I am hurt that I wasn't given the chance
To love you longer

DAYDREAMING FOREVER

Sometimes I lay in the dark
And imagine a life with you
Grey hair and wrinkled skin
A full life lived together

I imagine you still spinning me around the house
Whenever our song would play
And taking drives to unfamiliar places
Simply because we're bored

I imagine this beautiful life
Full of love and happiness
And then I'm brought back to reality
Where you no longer exist

The life I wish we had gotten
Exists only in my mind
And I wish
I could live in it forever

THE QUESTION THAT HAUNTS ME

You know
Sometimes when I think back
I think of all of the laughter and love
And to this day it still brings tears to my eyes
I think of moments shared and memories made
Smiles that could brighten the darkest of days
And hugs that could melt the pain away
I think of you and I
And our beautiful yet heartbreakingly short life together
All of the ups and downs
The good days and the bad
Not one time did my love for you waver
And your love for me shown in everything you did
When I think back on it all
I'm met with conflicting emotions
Happiness and warmth from being loved by you
Grief from losing the other half of my heart
Guilt from not being able to save you
And heartbreaking confusion from you leaving
I loved you with everything I had
Gave you my whole heart
And let you in to the deepest and darkest parts of my soul
I will always wonder why
Why you left
And why I wasn't enough for you to want to stay

THE SONG MY SHATTERED HEART SINGS

I heard a song today
Turns out you know it too
You spun me around the kitchen singing
I Can't Help Falling In Love With You

We smiled until our cheeks hurt
And sang the song together
I knew in that moment this song was ours
From now until forever

Every time the song would play
Whether it was on purpose or not
You'd take me by the hands and dance
Like it was your only thought

You'd stop in the middle of practice
Or your favorite video game
To dance with me no matter where
Even in the rain

Now I try to avoid it
Listening to our song
With you not being here with me
It just feels really wrong

I heard our song today
It's been 3 years at least
But you're not here to spin me around
All the dancing ceased

MOONLIGHT APOLOGIES

Stories untold
Never to be spoken
I wish I could forget
That they were ever real

Conversations we had
Haunt me
They follow me around
And torture me

Nobody knows
And I will never tell
I will carry this guilt
Until the very end

Although I know
I couldn't have changed your mind
I can't shake the feeling
That I just didn't try hard enough

I loved you more than anything
But it wasn't enough
I should've done more
I should've tried harder

The signs were there
Why didn't I see them?
I should've known
I should've done something

I so desperately wanted to believe you
When you promised you'd be okay
I chose to ignore the signs
And trust your words

I'm sorry
I am so profoundly sorry
I couldn't save you
And I'll never forgive myself

WILL YOU BLAME ME

Will you blame me?
If I never forget you
If I never move on with someone new
If I never let go of the things
That remind me of you

Will you blame me?
If I lay in bed all day
Because thoughts of you
Strangled my motivation to do anything else
And now I can't breathe

Will you blame me?
If thoughts of living
Feel like dying
And thoughts of dying
Feel like living

Will you blame me?
If I cry myself to sleep some nights
Then paint a smile on my face in the morning
If I say I'm okay
When honestly I'm the furthest thing from it

If I can't keep my promise to you
Will you blame me?

GUILTY

It all feels wrong
To smile
To laugh
Everything

I feel horrible
For finding joy in things
For making future plans
For making memories

The world feels empty
Without you in it
This air is too thick
To breathe on my own

You once told me
You wanted me to live
I'm trying
But it's hard

It was never supposed to be this way
You promised me
That you'd be okay
At least you're at peace now

People always tell me I'm strong
That I can get through this
But they fail to realize
That the guilt is eating me alive

It's not right
That you're not here
And I feel guilty
For living

MAYBE

When the light threatened to swallow me
The darkness held me close
How I've made it to today
Well I don't really know

Beaten, bruised, and broken
Are how I've lived thus far
The temporary happiness
Has left a permanent scar

Quiet screams in darkened rooms
Where nobody can hear
But secret wishes to the sky
That someone might be near

Dried tears on pillowcases
And words left unsaid
Wishing I could let it out
But everyone's in bed

So here I lay night after night
Drowning in worries and thoughts
Maybe someday I'll escape
Or maybe I will not

NO GOODBYE FOR MY HAUNTED HEART

Did you know
That hearts make a sound when they break?
It's a sound more haunting than any other
And one you can never unhear

This broken heart of mine
Stalks me like my shadow
Never ceasing
Even when the sun goes down

In the daylight
It walks behind me
And in the darkness
It holds me close

The pain I felt that day
Finds its way back to me
Every day like this
When I am encompassed by your memory

It's still hard sometimes
To accept that you're really gone
And as much as I hate goodbyes
I wish we had gotten one

BREAK NOW

I've heard that the eyes are the windows to the soul
I've also heard that you can see one's true heart through their eyes
Our eyes tell our stories
Even the one's we've tried desperately to bury

There's a reason I don't like eye contact
I'm afraid of what may be revealed
And I've fought too hard for too long
To break now

LIVE

I want to die
I want to leave this world
I want to be free
I don't want to hurt anymore

I want to be happy
I want to smile
I want to laugh
I want to not feel guilty for doing those

I want to forget about the past
I want to not stress over the future
I want to have no more worries
And no more fears

I want to chase my dreams
I want to travel the world
I want to try new things
And be who I've always wanted to be

I want to die
But I can't
Because in this life
I want to live

STEVEN

A moment
All it took was one moment
One glance
To know you would be someone so important

The start of the rest of my life
Brought me the greatest gift
A friendship so deep
Predestined to last a lifetime

There was no awkward phase
No uncomfortable moments
We fell into sync
Like we had been there all along

You took one look at this beaten and bruised soul
And never even flinched
Instead you showed me compassion and love
And a life I never knew could exist

To call you my best friend
Would be an understatement
You are more than that
More than family

You are another part of me
A song my soul sings along to
A poem my heart beats to the rhythm of
A story unmatched by any other

I will never be able to thank you enough
For every single thing
Every moment we have shared
Together and apart

You give me reason
Our friendship is my strength
I love you so much
Anam Cara

SYDNEY

I don't know where I'd be
Without you
You have been my rock
And my confidant

I tell you things
I find hard to admit to myself
You never judge me
Or make me feel like a let down

You have always supported me
Believed in me
And encouraged me
To pursue my dreams

You mean more to me
Than you'll ever know
And I know that without a doubt
You'll be there if I need you

I will never be able
To thank you enough
For everything that you've done for me
But I hope this can be a start

You're more than a friend to me
And closer than family
You're one of the main reasons
I still fight to live

STAR-KISSED WORLD

The wind whispers to me
Among the leaves of the trees
And the soil sings to me
With each step I take
Barefoot on the earth

Nighttime brings with it
My favorite piece of art
The night sky
Shimmering in a sea of stars
As the world falls asleep

This is the time
When I feel most alive
And maybe that's why
The concrete calls my name
Reaching out to draw me in

The city's night life
Has always intrigued me
Bringing me a sense of belonging
And a sense of peace
Much like stars in the night sky

City lights shine brightly
Painting their own picture
This is the place
Where the stars kiss the earth
And these stars I can touch

DREAM

The moon snuggles closely
With the stars in the night sky
The wind whispers sweetly
To the leaves in the trees

The sun softly kisses
The world and those within it
The beauty of life is all around
Yet I find solace in the night

In those moments
When the world has gone dark
And the silence of the world
Brings me comfort

I feel free
Finally at peace
And I can write away
My problems

Words flow effortlessly
From my fingertips
It's almost as though
They were created there

I feel compelled
To put my thoughts on paper
So I never lose them
Or forget what they once were

Putting my thoughts on paper
Is just my kind of therapy
It's what I want most
This is my dream

www.ingramcontent.com/pod-product-compliance
Lightning Source LLC
Chambersburg PA
CBHW032005060426
42449CB00031B/615